… NEW …

Shoelaces
and other stories

Hannie Truijens

Illustrated by Nina O'Connell

Sorry, wrong door page 2

The car race page 10

Shoelaces page 18

Nelson

Sorry, wrong door

Sam asked Meg and Deb to come to a big party in the hotel.
They were looking for him.
"I think it is this door,"
said Deb.
"Get on my back and have a look,"
said Meg.

"Sorry, wrong door," said Deb.
"We are looking for Sam the fox," said Meg.
"He is having a big party."
"Sam is not here," said Mr Giraffe.
"I will help you look for him."

Meg, Deb and Mr Giraffe went to the next door.
"I think it is this door," said Deb.
"Get down and have a look," said Meg.

"Sorry, wrong door," said Deb.
"We are looking for Sam the fox," said Meg.
"He is having a big party."
"Sam is not here," said Mrs Snake.
"I will help you look for him."

Meg, Deb, Mr Giraffe and Mrs
Snake went to the next door.
"I think it is this door,"
said Deb.
"Let me have a look," said Meg.

"Sorry, wrong door," said Meg.
"We are looking for Sam the fox," said Deb.
"He is having a big party."
"Sam is not here," said Mr Lion.
"I will help you look for him."

Meg, Deb, Mr Giraffe, Mrs Snake
and Mr Lion went to the next door.
"Sam is here," said Mr Giraffe.
"Yes, he is," said Mrs Snake.
"Yes, he is," said Mr Lion.

Sam opened the door.

"Hello, Meg and Deb," he said.

"Do your friends also want to come to my party?"

"Yes, please," said Mr Giraffe, Mrs Snake and Mr Lion.

The car race

The friends all have a car, but who has the best car?
"Let's have a race," they said.
"We will see who has the best car."

BANG went the gun.
Off went the friends.
Sam is in front with his long car.
"I will win this race," he said.

Clang, CLANG, **CLANG**, went
Sam's car.
Now Jip is in front with his
fast car.
"I will win this race," he said to Sam.

Rattle, RATTLE, **RATTLE**, went Jip's car.
Now Ben is in front with his tall car.
"I will win this race," he said to Jip.

Bump, BUMP, **BUMP**, went Ben's car.
Now Meg is in front with her
strong car.
"I will win this race," she said to Ben.

Squeak, SQUEAK, **SQUEAK**, went Meg's car.
Now Deb is in front with her small car.
"I will win this race," she said to Meg.

Brrrm, BRRRM, **BRRRM**, went Deb's car.
"My car is the best," she said.
"I will win this race."

"I did win the race," said Deb.
"My car was the best.
But not any more."

Shoelaces

Ben had new shoes.
New shoes for his front feet and his back feet.

Ben walked down the road, but
his back shoes stepped
on the laces of his front shoes.
Ben fell on his nose.
"Woof," he said.

Ben walked back to front, but
his front shoes stepped
on the laces of his back shoes.
Ben fell on his tail.
"Wooof," he said.

Ben walked to the side, but
his left shoes stepped
on the laces of his right shoes.
Ben fell on his side.
"Woooof," he said.

Ben walked to the other side,
but his right shoes stepped on
the laces of his left shoes.
Ben fell on his other side.
"Wooooof," he said.

"Let me tie your shoelaces for you," said Jip.
Jip tied all Ben's shoelaces.
Ben walked down the road.
"Woooooof," he said.

Ben took off his left shoes and his right shoes, his front shoes and his back shoes.

"Who needs shoes?" he said.